SEMPER FI

Michael Brady

BROADWAY PLAY PUBLISHING INC
224 E 62nd St, NY, NY 10065
www.broadwayplaypub.com
info@broadwayplaypub.com

SEMPER FI

© Copyright 1988 Michael Brady

All rights reserved. This work is fully protected under the copyright laws of the United States of America. No part of this publication may be photocopied, reproduced, stored in a retrieval system, or transmitted, in any form or by any means, electronic, mechanical, recording, or otherwise, without the prior permission of the publisher. Additional copies of this play are available from the publisher.

Written permission is required for live performance of any sort. This includes readings, cuttings, scenes, and excerpts. For amateur and stock performances, please contact Broadway Play Publishing Inc. For all other rights please contact Paradigm, 140 Broadway, NY NY 10005, 212 897-6400.

Cover art by Lyon Design

First edition: September 1988
This edition: October 2017
I S B N: 978-0-88145-062-0

Book design: Marie Donovan
Typeface: Palatino

ORIGINAL PRODUCTION

SEMPER FI opened 18 June 1987 at the Gloucester Stage Company, Gloucester MA. It was directed by Grey Cattell Johnson; the set and lighting design was by Lawrence Novakov-Lawlor; the costume design was by Jeanine Phaneuf Burgess; the production coordinator was Patrick J Scully; and the stage manager was Frederick Hahn.

GENERAL SAMUEL DAVIS	Guy Strauss
COLONEL OWEN CORBETT	Jim Mohr
DENNIS HARPER	Kelvin Keraga
LIEUTENANT ARTHUR JENKINS	Oliver Solomon
BRIAN CORBETT	Mark H Rogers
ANNE CORBETT	Manette Jungels
AGNES CORBETT	Frances West

DEDICATION

For the 237 Marines who died in Beirut, 23 October 1983

AUTHOR'S NOTE

SEMPER FI received an honorable mention in the 1985 CBS/Dramatists Guild national playwriting competition from the Virginia Stage Company. The play has benefitted additionally by readings by The Gloucester Stage Company, the Ensemble Studio Theater, and the Vietnam Veterans Theater Company. Special thanks are given to Liz Diggs and Israel Horovitz for their criticism and advice.

While suggested by actual events, the characters and situations of this play are the creation of the author.

CHARACTERS

OWEN CORBETT -- mid-forties, colonel, Marine Corps, career soldier

BRIAN CORBETT -- late-twenties, veterinarian, married to Anne. He is Owen's son.

ANNE CORBETT -- late-twenties, television news reporter, Canadian

AGNES CORBETT -- ex-wife of Owen

ARTY JENKINS -- late-twenties, Marine lieutenant

SAMUEL DAVIS -- mid-to-late fifties, general, Marine Corps

DENNIS HARPER -- a lawyer with the State Department

Setting: The country home of Brian and Anne; Marine Command Headquarters, Beirut; Committee Room, Washington D.C.

ACT ONE

Scene One

(A featureless, gray room, metal table, chairs, and a tape recorder. Seated at the table are GENERAL DAVIS, *in a Marine uniform, and* DENNIS HARPER, *a lawyer with the State Department. Standing in front of them is* COLONEL OWEN CORBETT, *and* ARTY (ARTHUR) JENKINS. *Both are dressed in combat uniforms.)*

DAVIS: *(Leaning over tape recorder, to* OWEN*)* Owen, you do understand, once I press this red button, every word is official?

OWEN: I know, Sam.

DAVIS: This will all go on your record. What do you say, Owen, withdraw your request.

OWEN: Can't you back me up on this, Sam?

DAVIS: No, I can't. And the rules of engagement are not going to be changed. Owen, maybe we can work something out here, but let's keep this in the family. You understand?

OWEN: I've got to go by the book.

HARPER: The man is not going to change his mind. Let's get on with it.

DAVIS: *(Pressing record button)* Special Deployment Forces, Marine Corps, Marine Amphibious Unit, standing orders review. Requested by forces commander. Present: General Samuel Davis, Marine Corps executive staff; Dennis Harper, State Department liaison, and Colonel Corbett, Classified, eyes only, transcript. Command Headquarters, Beirut... Colonel Corbett, you are requesting changes in the rules of engagement?

OWEN: Yes Sir.

DAVIS: The current rules are inadequate?

OWEN: Under the existing guidelines, I cannot protect my unit. I'm not allowed to initiate fire at hostiles. I'm not even cleared to return fire.

HARPER: You are in a highly populated area.

OWEN: There are civilians, and traffic, yes.

DAVIS: You understood the logic of this mission when it was assigned to you?

OWEN: Yes, Sir.

DAVIS: You are here to provide a presence for the civilian population. Presence, not control. Give these people some time to get back to normal, some time to pull together a stable and friendly government.

HARPER: Colonel, we are aware that you've taken casualties. But you must realize that this is primarily a diplomatic, not a military, initiative.

DAVIS: You're here as a manager, Colonel, a manager. Your unit is not, nor must it ever appear to be, combat ready. The current rules of engagement reflect that condition.

OWEN: My whole perimeter is porous. My guards can't even have their ammo locked and loaded in their guns.

DAVIS: *(Reading from a memo)* To minimize the very real risk of civilian casualties if weapons fire is not strictly controlled. You've requested anti-tank missiles, armor-piercing ordinance, early return of fire...

OWEN: ... All of which is called for by our position.

DAVIS: Your position, Colonel, is to win these people over. Create the impression of situation normal.

OWEN: Nothing is normal here, Sir. I have a growing morale problem. I'm taking casualties on every patrol. If I can't initiate fire, then I must have heavily fortified positions.

HARPER: Colonel, we can't give the appearance of an American military occupation. That's a dangerously wrong impression.

OWEN: I can't protect my command with impressions, Mr. Harper. I must have control of that access road. I need barriers and tank traps to block vehicle access.

HARPER: That access road is a major public highway, Colonel. There's only two in the entire country.

OWEN: I must control that road to insure the safety of my command.

(Pause; HARPER and DAVIS confer.)

DAVIS: Colonel, we have considered your suggestions, and at this time we see no need to change the rules of engagement.

OWEN: I ask that my proposals be submitted further up the chain of command.

DAVIS: Noted. *(Pressing the pause button on the recorder)*

HARPER: What are you doing?

DAVIS: Look, the man is my friend.

HARPER: There will be a gap in the tape.

DAVIS: I pushed the damn pause button. The tape isn't going anywhere.

HARPER: This is very irregular.

DAVIS: The colonel and I go back a long way. I don't think the man understands what's happening here. So just give me some slack, all right?

HARPER: All right.

DAVIS: *(To OWEN)* You're trying to go over my head, for Christ's sake?

OWEN: Sam, my tactical position...

DAVIS: You are not in a damn tactical position. You're in the capital of a friendly country. You're not landing on Iwo Jima. You are to demonstrate that order is emerging from this chaos. You are here, your command is here, to show presence, in the strict military sense of the term.

OWEN: We're doing that, Sam. We're visible. I've got the flag on our uniforms, our bunkers, on every jeep I send out on patrol. But it's a new game over here, Sam. There's a new crowd in town. Intelligence is sighting terrorists by the bus load. We're not a presence, Sam. We're a target.

HARPER: Colonel, you have the support of the legitimate government here.

OWEN: That government is just another faction, Mr. Harper. And the closer we get to them, the bigger a target we become.

HARPER: Our expectation, our perception, is that the Amphibious Unit is not a target.

OWEN: Your perception? These factions...

HARPER: Yes, these factions want to eliminate each other, but we're not part of that.

OWEN: Mr. Harper, they hate us. They hate everything about us. That's the only thing they agree on.

HARPER: Colonel, if you give the impression of digging in, of taking over, of occupying a part of this country, then you increase the likelihood of attack. Create the impression of neutrality and you minimize the risk of attack. That is your best defense.

OWEN: Mr. Harper, Sam, would you look around you? This is not a place that runs on logic, or words. No impression is going to protect us. Let me alter the rules of engagement. At least let me lock and load. You're spiking my guns!

DAVIS: Negative, we've been through that. What are you telling us? The mission has changed?

ACT ONE

OWEN: The conditions of the mission have changed, yes.

DAVIS: You know who has a hand in over here? The Secretaries of State, Defense, the Navy, the Pentagon, and the National Security Council. All that weight has scrutinized the rules of engagement. You think some lieutenant colonel is going to change things? This is what has always held you back, Owen. You don't comprehend reality. This is out of your hands. You are inches away from being relieved of duty. Am I right, Mr. Harper?

HARPER: *(To* OWEN*)* I would have to agree, Colonel.

DAVIS: So the question is simple, do you want the command?

OWEN: I want to protect my command

DAVIS: Do you want the command? No changes in the rules of engagement.

OWEN: Give me control over that access road, Sam. If I can't block that road I can't secure my position. I can't even guarantee security in this command bunker.

DAVIS: No way. That's I-95 out there. We've got to have the appearance of situation normal.

OWEN: You've got to give me this, Sam. Please. I want to protect my men.

DAVIS: *(Shouting)* And I don't, you son of a bitch? I'm going to order you out. Do you want the command, as is, no changes, yes or no?

OWEN: Yes. Yes, I want the command.

DAVIS: Then that's how we handle this. All right. *(Pressing the record button)* Colonel Corbett, you understand that there will be no changes in the rules of engagement?

OWEN: Yes, Sir.

DAVIS: Do you have anything further to add?

OWEN: No, Sir.

DAVIS: This meeting is concluded. *(Turns off recorder.)* Well, we have all just covered our precious behinds. Damn it, Owen, do you know how many buttons I pushed to get you this very visible command? Now I look like a damned fool.

OWEN: You know I'm right, Sam.

DAVIS: Listen up. You're job here is to manage this situation, to sit tight, and hunker down, period. Owen, you made yourself look bad, on the record. And you made me look bad. I was wrong about you. You're a light colonel, pure and simple. You're not suited for higher rank. *(He exits.)*

OWEN: Mr. Harper, you could authorize me to cut that access road.

HARPER: Sorry, Colonel. The security arrangement is a military decision. I have to follow procedures. *(He exits.)*

OWEN: Well, Arty, we have heard the voice from the top of the mountain.

ARTY: Sir, shall I issue an order to lock and load? *(Pause)*

OWEN: Negative, Lieutenant

ARTY: I could make it my call, Sir.

OWEN: No, Arty. Like Mr. Harper, I have to follow procedures.

(The lights gradually dim. The sound of a truck is heard, as though from a distance, gradually increasing in speed. The sound abruptly cuts out. Lights down.)

Scene Two

(The first floor of an older, Victorian style house, recently renovated. Downstage is a wooden deck bordered by a vegetable garden and shrubs in a neat row. The house has a modern kitchen with an open dining area, a living room with contemporary art work prominently displayed, as well as a state-of-the-art video monitor, with a VCR, and a study with a built-in bookcase displaying a collection of veterinary texts and a large chart showing an anatomical cut-away of a horse, revealing bones, organs, and muscles in layers of plastic. BRIAN *enters, carrying several large cardboard boxes which he puts in the study.* BRIAN *exits and then returns quickly, carrying an easel and a large official-issue map of the Korean peninsula, circa 1950, illustrating the path of MacArthur's amphibious invasion marked by large blue arrows.* BRIAN *sets the map on the easel, and begins to remove books from the boxes.* ANNE *enters, carrying a briefcase slung over her shoulders. She is casually dressed, wearing well-worn designer running shoes.)*

ANNE: Hello.

BRIAN: Hi. *(They kiss.)*

ANNE: What is going on here, Brian? Our study looks like a flea market.

BRIAN: I brought a few things down from the attic. I thought Dad might appreciate seeing some familiar things down here.

ANNE: Sounds like the old family deception to me. *(Paging through book)* Davey Crockett, Frontier Hero?

BRIAN: I had the approved American childhood.

ANNE: Hmm, I wouldn't mind seeing you in a coonskin cap, if you catch my drift. *(They kiss.* ANNE *crosses to TV monitor.)* Any word from your father?

BRIAN: What?

ANNE: *(Puts tape into VCR.)* Did your father call again? It's been a week.

BRIAN: No. If he said three o'clock tomorrow afternoon, that's when he'll be here.

ANNE: *(Noticing the map)* What is that?

BRIAN: A battle map of Korea, official issue. Here's MacArthur's amphibious landing. *(Pointing)* And here, just south of Inchon, is where my father went in. His first time in combat.

ANNE: I know the feeling. *(Takes notebook from briefcase, begins making notes.)* Henry had me doing Marine-in-the-street interviews today.

BRIAN: That sounds like Henry.

ANNE: I had this one crew-cut charmer who stared at me like I was on the menu at Burger King. The network picked up the segment.

BRIAN: Good for you.

ANNE: Yeah. *(Runs segment of tape.)* Henry's got word the bodies are being flown in tomorrow. That's the big story. That and your father. And his whereabouts.

BRIAN: We have a deal, don't we?

ANNE: CBS led with your father last night.

BRIAN: So?

ANNE: So your father is big news. He's the biggest story in the whole country. If I could get him on camera...

BRIAN: No way, Annie! No questions, no interviews. This house is a safe harbor. End of story.

ACT ONE

ANNE: Brian, give me fifteen minutes with him.

BRIAN: No.

ANNE: Let him defend himself. I might be able to help him. If he was responsible for what happened ...

BRIAN: He's not. I know my father.

ANNE: Oh Brian, you spend all day in the stable with your horses and your cows. I'm out there in the trenches. If your father's responsible, he will need to defend himself. And if he's not responsible, then he'd better get his story out, and fast. Because in the living rooms of America he is coming across as the man who screwed up. He's the perfect scapegoat. He may want to talk.

BRIAN: He doesn't. Look, Annie, he's my Dad. He's family. And with family you draw ranks. That's what families are for.

ANNE: I'm not sure this is such a great idea, your father staying with us.

BRIAN: Annie, what are you talking about?

ANNE: Brian, I come home and you're re-arranging the furniture.

BRIAN: Just a few books.

ANNE: And you're fighting the Korean War in our living room. Brian, if I can't be who I am, say what's on my mind in my own home, then I think your father should stay with your uncle. Bewley is always going on about how he never gets to see him.

BRIAN: Annie, this is my father's house.

ANNE: No, this is our home, yours and mine. Or what are all those mortgage payments about?

BRIAN: Annie, he's my father. And I'm all he's got right now.

ANNE: I never know what to say to him. He's so damn military. "We do this, then we do that, then boom, ba, boom,

boom." Like when your sister starts in about standing tall for America. I want to dig a fall-out shelter.

BRIAN: *(Picks up empty boxes.)* My father's not like that. *(BRIAN exits into the house.)*

ANNE: So what is he like? Brian?

(ANNE exits, following BRIAN. The lights dim in the house. The lights come up on the far end of the deck. OWEN and ARTY enter, dressed in casual clothes, not uniforms. ARTY carries two large duffel bags.)

OWEN: You're certain we lost those photographers?

ARTY: Twenty miles back.

OWEN: Good. *(Turns to face the house.)* Well, this is it.

ARTY: Looks nice.

OWEN: New paint. You remember the old paint? You and Tim did a fine job.

ARTY: Three coats. Oil base.

OWEN: Tim was a good worker. This hedge is new. And this deck, brand new. *(Feeling the deck with his hand)* I wonder if he did this himself. I don't remember him being handy.

ARTY: Nice work.

OWEN: I had always visualized a pool here, diving board, tiles all around. *(ARTY makes a move toward the house.)* Whoa, whoa, where are you pointed?

ARTY: I thought I'd get this show on the road.

OWEN: Yeah? Maybe you'd like to have your clock personally cleaned. Get back down here, young fellow. *(ARTY moves away from the house.)* First explore the terrain. Observation, intelligence, then appropriate action.

ARTY: So this is observation?

OWEN: Right.

ACT ONE 11

ARTY: I thought observation was driving past the house four times.

OWEN: That was site verification.

ARTY: Uh-huh.

OWEN: The last time I was out here, Agnes and I parted company. I never imagined I'd see that day. I wish everything didn't look so damned new. I need a moment here, to verify how to proceed.

ARTY: "Look ahead for progress, not back for precedent."

OWEN: Now what the hell is that?

ARTY: A quote. One of your quotes.

OWEN: You mean you actually learned something at Amphibious Warfare School? You just gave me chapter and verse from the Tentative Manual for Landing Operations.

ARTY: Feels like we are in the middle of one tentative landing, Sir.

OWEN: Well, you're right there.

(The lights come back up in the study. BRIAN *and* ANNE *enter.* BRIAN *carries a large cardboard box.)*

BRIAN: Dad was always tougher on Bobby. He was the oldest. For Dad it was always Bobby this, Bobby that. Bobby, Bobby, Bobby. And of course Sukie could do no wrong. She had memorized every Marine battle by the time she was six. I was that very lucky child---born right in the middle. Everyone ignored me

ANNE: *(Moving toward the deck, looking out toward* ARTY *and* OWEN*)* Your mother says you were always even tempered. Oh my God.

BRIAN: What's the matter?

ANNE: He's here.

BRIAN: Who's here?

ANNE: He, him. Your father.

BRIAN: *(Looking out to deck)* What's he doing here?

ANNE: You're asking me?

BRIAN: *(Runs back to study, opens large cardboard box.)* This isn't like him.

ANNE: Well, Mr. Punctuality is here a day early. And there's somebody with him. Does your father have a bodyguard?

BRIAN: *(Removes a large, handmade wooden clock from the box; hangs the clock on the wall.)* I've got to get this up.

ANNE: What are you doing? What is that thing?

BRIAN: It's a clock.

ANNE: It's an ugly clock. And why are you putting it on our wall?

BRIAN: *(Pulling a clock key from the box, checking the time on his wristwatch.)* My father is very fond of this clock. His uncle made it by hand. *(Winds the clock.)*

ANNE: *(Listening)* It's ticking.

BRIAN: *(Picking up cardboard boxes, running to the kitchen to hide them out of sight.)* That's what clocks do. I found it in the attic.

ANNE: That's probably where your mother stuffed it. And where it belongs.

BRIAN: Think of it as possessing sentimental value.

ANNE: It possesses ugly value. That thing will distort the whole room. Take it down!

BRIAN: He'll be expecting to see it.

ANNE: Brian Boru Corbett!

BRIAN: Don't call me Brian Boru. You know I don't like to use my middle name.

ANNE: Well, Dad's expecting to come home to the warrior king of Ireland. I don't want to disappoint him.

ACT ONE

BRIAN: Annie, so help me...

(Lights come up full on OWEN *and* ARTY.*)*

ARTY: You sure you don't want to go in alone on this one?

OWEN: Just stay on the point for a while, till we're all at our ease.

ARTY: Keep the conversation general.

OWEN: Right.

ARTY: Food, the weather, sports, nice place you got here...

OWEN: That's the plan.

ARTY: Got it.

ANNE: I'm not ready for this.

BRIAN: Neither am I, but let's go out there and greet my father, okay? Don't mention the bombing unless he does, and stay off politics. *(They move toward the deck.)*

ARTY: Maybe we should have called?

OWEN: That's all right. We're coming home to family.

ARTY: And family adjusts.

OWEN: You're learning, Lieutenant.

*(*BRIAN *and* ANNE *cross down to the deck.* BRIAN *and* OWEN *embrace. A long pause.)*

BRIAN: Damn, it's good to see you, Dad.

OWEN: Good to see you, Son.

BRIAN: You're a little early. We weren't expecting...

OWEN: ... thought we'd use the extra day.

BRIAN: That's great, great. *(To* ARTY*)* Brian...

ARTY: Arty.

(They shake hands.)

ANNE: *(Stepping forward.)* Owen, hello. It's good to see you again.

OWEN: *(Shaking ANNE's hand)* Anne, it's been a long time, hasn't it. Well, you're keeping well. This here is Arty.

ARTY: *(Shaking hands.)* Arthur Jenkins, M'am.

OWEN: Thought I'd show this young fellow a bit of the world.

ARTY: I know you probably weren't expecting two of us, M'am.

ANNE: That's all right.

OWEN: *(To* BRIAN*)* This deck is something. You bring in a carpenter?

BRIAN: No, this is all me.

ARTY: *(To* ANNE*)* If there isn't room, M'am, I can hit the base.

ANNE: We have lots of room, but if you call me M'am again, I'll lock you in the basement.

ARTY: Pleased to meet you, Anne.

OWEN: I didn't know you knew carpentry.

BRIAN: I taught myself, a while back.

OWEN: And this hedge. That's new. *(To* ANNE*)* I bet this is your project?

ANNE: My little contribution to the war effort. I mean, yes, my hedge. *(Pause)*

ARTY: Uhm, nice place you got here, M'am. I mean Anne. It's very...green.

ANNE: Arty Arthur Jenkins, we seem to have a refrigerator full of Canadian beer, the only really civilized beer in the world, but perhaps I'm slightly prejudiced. Maybe you'd help us plow a path through them.

ARTY: Well, if I could be of some small assistance.

BRIAN: I'll show you where, Arty, then you help yourself. House rules.

ACT ONE 15

ARTY: Okay, but first I'll get our gear in.

BRIAN: I'll give you a hand.

ARTY: I can manage. *(Picks up a duffel.)*

BRIAN: *(Picking up the other bag.)* Welcome home, Dad.

OWEN: Thanks, Son.

(ARTY *and* BRIAN *cross into the house and exit.)*

OWEN: You have done a lot of work out here. It shows.

ANNE: Thanks.

OWEN: The feel of the place is different. That's only natural.

ANNE: There must be a lot of memories for you here.

OWEN: Yes, Agnes and I, we had some history here. She always wanted pine trees. Hard to grow them down here, though I never really tried. Well, a new hedge and a new deck, gives the place some definition.

ANNE: Owen, I... this will probably come out all wrong. I'm sorry about... I know it must have been terrible for you over there.

OWEN: Terrible for everyone.

ANNE: You must have lost friends. I... Brian told me not to talk about it.

OWEN: I did lose some friends. I lost some good boys.

ANNE: And you should know that while you're here, no one at the station knows that you're in this house. That's my agreement with Brian.

OWEN: Thanks. I'm not all that fond of the media at the moment.

ANNE: Right.... Well, let's get you sorted away. Then I'll give you a proper tour, show you round and about. We'll put you in Bobby's old room. That's the biggest. And Arty can have the spare.

OWEN: You must see Agnes. I know she stayed nearby.

(BRIAN *re-enters from the house, crossing to the deck.*)

ANNE: Agnes is a sweetheart.

OWEN: Is she still keeping well?

BRIAN: Dad, stop pumping Annie for information.

OWEN: I am not pumping.

BRIAN: Yes, you are.

ANNE: I'll start dinner. (*She crosses back into the kitchen.*)

BRIAN: Look, Dad, Mom won't visit the house while you're here.

OWEN: I thought this time she might make an exception.

BRIAN: That's how things are. I called Bobby.

OWEN: How's he doing?

BRIAN: He's all right. But I wouldn't count on Bobby showing up, either. Sukie is talking to her CO, trying to get an emergency leave.

OWEN: She won't get one.

BRIAN: So, it's you and me, Dad.

OWEN: Is your mother still with that Phillip fellow?

BRIAN: Yeah, she's with Phil. And Dad, if you have any questions about Mom, ask me, not Annie, all right?

OWEN: Someone make you the CO around here? You giving the orders now?

BRIAN: It's not an order, Dad. But let's make it a house rule, okay?

OWEN: Well, I'll take that under advisement.

(BRIAN *exits into the house. The lights shift around* OWEN, *who remains on stage. The sound of an accelerating truck grows louder, then abruptly cuts out. Lights down.*)

Scene Three

(Later that night, after dinner. ARTY, ANNE, *and* BRIAN *sit in the living room, drinking coffee.* OWEN *remains on the deck.)*

ANNE: Some more coffee, Arty?

ARTY: No thanks, M'am...I mean Anne.

ANNE: How about another piece of pie?

ARTY: Don't mind if I do. Where are you from, up in Canada?

ANNE: Toronto. Go Blue Jays.

ARTY: You miss it?

ANNE: Oh, I regret not having the Queen and Lady Di over for tea.

ARTY: Is that a yes?

ANNE: Yes, I miss home. But I go where the company tells me to go.

ARTY: Oh yeah, I know that tune. You know what a fellow told me once? A Canadian is just an American who talks differently.

ANNE: Yeah, there are a few Yanks who think like that.

ARTY: This fellow was a Canadian himself.

ANNE: So I just walked into a little trap. How did you meet your Canadian cousin?

ARTY: Met him on maneuvers, north of the border.

ANNE: And where was that?

ARTY: Well, I'm not allowed to say.

BRIAN: *(Crosses to deck, hands* OWEN *a drink.)* Dad?

OWEN: Thanks, Son. You two always cook together?

BRIAN: Sometimes one or the other, it depends.

OWEN: Your mother and I were always snarling in the kitchen. (OWEN *and* BRIAN *cross to the living room.*)

BRIAN: I remember.

OWEN: She had to have things just so. Not that I couldn't cook, if it came to that.

BRIAN: You were the baker.

OWEN: That's right.

BRIAN: You taught me how to...

OWEN: A man should know how to bake bread.

BRIAN: Right.

OWEN: Your mother is a cook. She is not a baker.

BRIAN: We were getting worried about you.

OWEN: Now what's the first rule you learned as a kid? You don't worry about the old man.

BRIAN: It's been ten days since you called.

OWEN: We just took the leisure route.

BRIAN: Well, you're home now. You too, Arty.

ARTY: I'm much obliged.

(BRIAN *hands drink to* ARTY.)

ARTY: Thanks.

OWEN: *(To* BRIAN*)* Sukie tells me that Bobby's doing well.

BRIAN: We saw him last Christmas. He came down for a few days.

OWEN: He ask about me?

BRIAN: I try to keep him informed, when I know what you're doing.

ACT ONE

OWEN: Well, next time you talk to your brother, you tell him I've been thinking about him. Would you do that?

BRIAN: Sure, Dad.

ANNE: Bobby could sell ice to Eskimos, in bulk. Cheers. *(They all drink.)*

OWEN: I traced Sukie down last year, in Rota, Rota Spain. She's good, taking to it. The Mediterranean Fleet is a good position, very visible. She keeps putting in for carrier duty.

BRIAN: Suke's a little bulldog.

OWEN: *(To* ANNE*)* Carrier duty is combat classified, restricted for females. But she keeps requesting a transfer.

ANNE: I guess Sukie knows what she wants.

OWEN: When she first started in about the Naval Academy, I was opposed. She flanked me. Got her letter of recommendation, did all the tests. Sukie graduated seventeenth in her class. I still say any potential combat role is inappropriate for women, but Sukie, she's exceptional.

ARTY: *(To* ANNE*)* The Navy's different.

ANNE: How so?

ARTY: More genteel.

OWEN: Who gave you that information?

ARTY: A Navy captain.

OWEN: That figures.

BRIAN: *(Crossing to bookcase.)* Look what I found in the attic.

OWEN: God, your old Black Stallion books. These must be worth something now. And the Atlas. This must be thirty years old. And the Shakespeares. *(To* ARTY*)* Now here's an education for you, young fellow. Not all that high-tech stuff. If you're going to take men into battle, give them hell and Henry.

ARTY: I'll store that.

OWEN: *(Reading)* "...who fights with me today will be my brother..." Of course today it's "... he who computer simulates with me." You see, we're not fighters anymore. No, we are managers, managing situations for other managers, and so on. You remember that, young fellow, next time you're out there on the electronic battlefield.

ARTY: Will do.

OWEN: That's where you're headed. They've got these robot tanks and these robot jets, and it's just a matter of time before they put a little robot brain in your head, and then, bleep, off you go to war whistling little robot songs.

ARTY: No way.

OWEN: *(Puts book back on shelf.)* That so? You'll just be another robot blip on the robot screen.

ARTY: They can change the instrument, might change the tactics, but they will still need the man.

ANNE: We do have some new books.

OWEN: *(To* BRIAN*)* Right, your animal books.

ANNE: *(To* ARTY*)* I think every home needs a few good animal books, don't you, Arty?

ARTY: Right.

OWEN: *(Reading the spine of a textbook.) Vertebrate Muscular Structure* by Brian Corbett. That's an accomplishment son. How many of these have you written?

BRIAN: Three all together.

ANNE: And a contract for number four. Tell your father about your promotion.

OWEN: What's this?

BRIAN: Well, the veterinary department just bumped me up to associate professor.

ACT ONE 21

OWEN: That's fine, Son. You move on up the chain. That's the way. You always knew what you wanted. Even when you were a kid with all those snails.

BRIAN: They were lizards, Dad.

OWEN: What?

BRIAN: Remember you brought me back those lizards from Japan?

OWEN: I don't recollect.

BRIAN: *(To* ARTY*)* My brother tried to poison them. My sister helped him.

OWEN: *(Noticing the clock)* Roger's clock. Isn't that something? Must be the last thing he put together before the landing. *(Putting his ear to the clock)* Still runs.

BRIAN: We keep it wound up.

OWEN: We stopped by Roger's grave a while back, Arty and I. *(To* BRIAN*)* You remember Omaha Beach? When did we take the family over there?

BRIAN: Summer of fifty-eight.

OWEN: You were ten.

BRIAN: That was Bobby. I was six.

OWEN: Right, right...Your mother always hated this clock. Roger was nineteen when he died. Killed in the last crusade. I like to think that Roger knew why he fought and why he died. His war had a goal, a purpose. Roger didn't die for public relations. Roger didn't die for presence. Someone gets careless. And men die. It's the oldest song in the book. *(Pause)*

ANNE: Another beer, Arty?

ARTY: Thanks.

OWEN: What was I saying?

BRIAN: Uncle Roger.

OWEN: He was a good man. They were all good men, all of them. All men of quality. Oh, God. I should have issued the order to lock and load.

ARTY: Sir?

ANNE: What do you mean, Owen? Didn't you have ammunition?

BRIAN: Annie, cool it.

OWEN: I walked the perimeter. I saw it coming. To hell with all of them. I should have adopted a tactical position.

ARTY: Colonel?

OWEN: I was the commanding officer. I was responsible. I should have cut that damned access road.

ANNE: What happened, Owen?

BRIAN: Annie, back off.

ANNE: Let your father talk. What about that access road, Owen?

BRIAN: Annie, I said back off, now you back off right now.

ARTY: Begging the colonel's pardon, but there are civilians present here, Sir. *(Pause)*

OWEN: Right. Thank you, Lieutenant. I may be damaged goods, but I am still classified.

BRIAN: Well, at least you're home. *(Pause)* Dad, I said you're home now.

OWEN: You know what they say. Home is the place where when you knock on the door, they've got to let you in. No matter what you smell like. Reminds me of... No, it doesn't remind me of a thing. (OWEN *crosses to the deck,* ARTY *following.)* You look tired, Lieutenant. Turn in.

ARTY: Yes, Sir. *(He crosses back into the house.)* I'm a guest in this house, but I've got to say this. I know what the man's been through... That was a great meal. I'm much obliged. Goodnight.

ACT ONE   23

BRIAN: Goodnight, Arty.

ANNE: Goodnight.

(ARTY *exits.*)

BRIAN: Annie, what the hell are you trying to pull? Lay off my father.

ANNE: Brian, I'm trying to help him.

BRIAN: We had an agreement while my father is in this house. Didn't we?

ANNE: Brian, your father is caught in something, something very ugly. You'd better make some phone calls and have a lawyer on hold.

BRIAN: You don't think for a minute he could be at fault in this?

ANNE: Brian, do you need a road map?

BRIAN: Annie, keep your voice down.

ANNE: I'm sorry.

BRIAN: For Christ's sake.

ANNE: I said I was sorry. *(Pause)* Brian, you're not six years old any more. Get your father a lawyer. (ANNE *exits.* BRIAN *crosses to the deck where* OWEN *is sitting. Neither talks for some time.*)

OWEN: I must be feeling that flight back here. No matter how many times you cross those time zones...

BRIAN: You were just talking.

OWEN: Talking. Old clocks. Old wars no one remembers. Just talk. There are times when I'm in a briefing, everyone else is quiet, and I just roll on and on. I always say something. Then I say it again, and again. I can't turn it off. I'm like the little boy who spelled banana. He got it right, but he couldn't stop. *(Spelling)* B-a-n-a-n-a-n-a-n... I don't know when to shut up. It's affected my promotions, I know. God forgive me. Those boys aren't even cold in the ground, and I'm worried about my career.

BRIAN: Sounds like you're being awfully hard on yourself.

OWEN: You don't know the half of it.

BRIAN: We have just one rule around here. You drink my booze; you say what's on your mind.

OWEN: The whole time I was over there, I knew with an abiding certainty that we were vulnerable to attack. I should have howled, screamed, anything. Maybe if I had, those boys would still be alive today. But I am a Company man, and I played by the Company rules. Now they're saying I didn't take necessary security precautions. They say I didn't protect my men. I won't take that. I won't!

BRIAN: Who is saying that?

OWEN: I've been in Washington. There's an investigation in progress. I can't talk about it.

BRIAN: Dad, I want to help you. What are they saying in Washington? Are there formal charges against you?

OWEN: Not yet. *(Pause)* Brian, I've been a Marine all my life. Never wanted to be anything else, just a good Marine. And the good ones bring their men home or die with them. *(Long pause.)*

BRIAN: Dad, Dad... I'm sure you did the best you could.

OWEN: Ah, just listen to me, yapping away again. Yap, yap, yap.

BRIAN: Do you still run your five miles?

OWEN: Every morning, Arty and I.

BRIAN: I thought tomorrow I'd tag along.

OWEN: That would be fine.

BRIAN: Well, I'd better help Annie, or I'll hear about it.

ACT ONE

OWEN: She's a good one. Loyal to you, all the way. That's a blessing. Your mother and I, we had a pact. Twenty-five years, the pension, up and out, then we'd find some nice pine trees to lie under. Well, that's history now. At least we have some time, you and I. I never had much time for you, or Bobby or Sukie when you were kids. Now there's all the time in the world. *(Pause)* Brian, they're going to take away my command.

BRIAN: What can you do?

OWEN: Not much. Sit tight. I just committed a security breach, telling you.

BRIAN: Then I never heard it from you. *(He starts to exit.)*

OWEN: I guess you can take Roger's clock down now.

BRIAN: Dad, you don't think...

OWEN: You go on in, son. I'll just make sure all the stars are present and accounted for.

BRIAN: Goodnight, Dad.

OWEN: Goodnight, Son.

(BRIAN enters the house, crosses to the study, removes the clock, and then exits. OWEN remains on stage. He looks skyward.) B-a-n-a-n-a-n-a-n...

(The lights shift. The sound of an accelerating truck gets louder, then cuts out. Lights down.)

Scene Four

(The lights shift around OWEN, *who remains on stage.* HARPER *enters, carrying the tape recorder from Scene One.* DAVIS *enters.* OWEN *waits for* DAVIS *to finish his interview with* HARPER.*)*

HARPER: *(His finger on the stop button.)* Thank you, General.

DAVIS: I would just like it understood...

HARPER: The committee will be contacting you. Unless you would care to make another statement for the record?

DAVIS: *(Standing)* No. *(He starts to exit, encounters* OWEN.*)* You remember what Truman said? If you want a friend in Washington, buy a dog. Watch your back in there, Owen.

(He exits. OWEN *crosses to* HARPER.*)*

HARPER: Please, sit down, Colonel. (HARPER *leafs through a manila folder.)* I'm sorry you've had to wait. The committee is running behind schedule. We've had several interviews today

OWEN: General Davis?

HARPER: We've questioned the general, yes. Before we begin, Colonel, let me just assure you that this is not a witch hunt. The committee is solely interested in the facts surrounding the attack on the Marine Amphibious Unit. We're not pointing any fingers.

OWEN: I'm glad to hear that.

HARPER: Colonel, some of this will be familiar ground, but the rules of evidence require that we follow this procedure.

OWEN: Understood.

ACT ONE

HARPER: I want to make absolutely sure you do understand, Colonel. Some of our previous discussion was off the record.

OWEN: I understand.

HARPER: This is to insure that everything is on the record.

OWEN: I said that I understand. Let's get this over with.

HARPER: *(Pressing record button)* Colonel Corbett, you've waived counsel for these preliminary questions?

OWEN: That is correct.

HARPER: If at any point you should desire legal counsel, a lawyer will be provided, without prejudice to you in this investigation.

OWEN: I'm prepared to answer your questions.

HARPER: Colonel, you were in command of the Special Forces?

OWEN: Yes, in command of the MAU, the Marine Amphibious Unit, yes.

HARPER: Colonel, were you aware of any security problems in your position prior to the attack?

OWEN: Well, as you knew...Yes, as a result of our patrolling, of our intelligence, we were, we knew we were in a less than secure position.

HARPER: Less than secure?

OWEN: No military environment is guaranteed secure, of course. But we lacked the basic ability to control our position, to provide minimum basic security. No control, no security.

HARPER: And you were aware of this lack of control?

OWEN: This was apparent. No rounds, no chambered rounds in the guard's guns. We couldn't lock and load. We were in a civilian zone.

HARPER: And that was a security problem?

OWEN: Yes, the rules of engagement...

HARPER: I'm not asking about the rules of engagement, Colonel, but about your awareness of basic security.

OWEN: I know, but the rules...

HARPER: Colonel, were you aware of a security risk due to the nearby access road?

OWEN: Yes, we have a public road there, heavy civilian traffic.

HARPER: And that was a security risk?

OWEN: Obviously. But the rules of engagement were such...

HARPER: Colonel, we're not examining the rules.

OWEN: The rules were such that we lived with this obvious problem.

HARPER: The access road?

OWEN: Yes.

HARPER: So you were aware of this problem with the access road?

OWEN: I said that, yes. Any fool could see... I mean, yes, anyone who was there could see that this highway ran right up to our position. No control.

HARPER: The Marine Amphibious Unit did not control this access road?

OWEN: The rules of...

HARPER: You did not control this access?

OWEN: No.

HARPER: Were you aware that your perimeter was susceptible to terrorist penetration?

OWEN: We had a public road out there.

HARPER: So you were aware that your perimeter was not secure. *(Pause)* Colonel?

OWEN: Yes. I was aware... I was aware.

ACT ONE

HARPER: And did you do anything to correct this problem?

OWEN: I brought my evaluation to the attention of my superiors.

HARPER: Did you do anything else to correct this security problem?

OWEN: I followed standard military procedure.

HARPER: Did you take any other action?

OWEN: No.

HARPER: In your mind, Colonel, do you think you did everything you could to protect your command?

OWEN: What?

HARPER: Do you feel that you did everything possible to protect your men?

OWEN: Everything? Given the circumstances. Given what happened. I...no.

HARPER: Colonel?

OWEN: No!

HARPER: *(Presses stop button)* Well, Colonel, that's all we need today.

OWEN: But I haven't explained it all.

HARPER: This is just a preliminary review.

OWEN: Damn it, the rules of engagement must be discussed.

HARPER: Colonel, the oversight committee at this time is only trying to assess your a priori knowledge of the status of your position.

OWEN: For God's sake, man, what are you saying to me?

HARPER: We want to know what you knew, and when. The rules of engagement are not the issue.

OWEN: Oh, no? Those rules and the people who thought up those rules are the whole damn problem.

HARPER: We'll be contacting you, Colonel.

OWEN: My command was destroyed because of those rules!

HARPER: If you will excuse me.

OWEN: Destroyed!

(HARPER exits. *The lights shift around* OWEN *who remains on stage. The sound of an accelerating truck is heard, growing louder, followed by an explosion, but muffled, as if coming from some distance. Lights down.)*

Scene Five

(The deck. Evening, quite late. The sounds of insects, cicadas, and night birds, owls. The stars are very bright and obvious. ANNE enters, dressed in a night robe. She sits. A long pause.)

OWEN: I used to sit out here, the first night after I got back. Of course there wasn't a deck then, just the grass. I'd try to sort things out, find some perspective.

ANNE: Do you always look for perspective at three in the morning?

OWEN: *(Pointing off-stage)* The raccoons used to pop out from over there.

ANNE: They still do.

OWEN: They won't if you're upwind.

(ANNE shifts, moving closer to OWEN.)

OWEN: Always stay downwind of the garbage.

ANNE: Now there's some words to live by.

OWEN: You like it down here?

ANNE: You mean the lower forty-eight?

OWEN: This part of the country.

ANNE: It's all right.

OWEN: You miss home, your folks?

ANNE: Oh we get up there when we can, when I can get away from the salt mines.

OWEN: You're a working girl-working woman. Sounds important to you.

ANNE: Oh I have a few good old boys who need some convincing that I'm alive and competent.

OWEN: You're a straight shooter.

ANNE: Maybe I am.

OWEN: That won't win you a lot of friends. *(Pause)* I do like the deck.

ANNE: Brian put a lot of care into it.

OWEN: He has discipline.

ANNE: Makes you sick, doesn't it?

OWEN: You want to have a family, kids? Maybe I'm getting out of line...

ANNE: That's all right. The jury's still deadlocked on that one...

OWEN: So, are you this new woman I've read so much about?

ANNE: Could be, evolution is pretty bumpy. *(Pause)*

OWEN: *(Looking skyward)* Somewhere up there is a satellite, spins 'round the earth twelve times every day. It has what they call a distant imaging device that can see layer after layer of the earth below. When it flies over England they can see villages that died out in the Middle Ages, wiped out by plague. In the Sahara they've seen settlements covered by the desert a thousand years ago. They pointed it over Central America, and that imaging device sent back the pattern of Mayan cities, dozens of them, and roads, and dams, a whole civilization, and all its civilized traces, lost in the rain forests...*Ouranou Asteroentos.*

ANNE: Is this a quiz?

OWEN: No quiz. 'The Starry Sky.' Homer.

ANNE: Homer?

OWEN: The writer. The "Iliad"?

ANNE: You mean old Penelope, sewing and unsewing?

ACT ONE 33

OWEN: Waiting for her man to come home, minus his companions. That Homer.

ANNE: One of the old guys.

OWEN: Probably several of the old guys.

ANNE: You cover a lot of ground

OWEN: Just bits and pieces. It's held me back.

ANNE: I don't understand.

OWEN: I'm considered "bookish." I tend to talk in complete sentences. And in my world that is viewed with suspicion. I should've stuck with tactics, left the philosophy to the civilians. I've gone as far as I'm going to fly.

ANNE: You don't look so decrepit.

OWEN: Thanks. I used to think I had it all figured out. God put us here with a plan in mind. We can't know the plan, but that's all right, because there is this plan. And we try to find our way, point by point, marker by marker, till we go as far as we can go, then someone else takes our place. That's what I've always thought... The stars are different over there, not by much, but different. I used to look for a pattern right there *(Pointing)*, a design like a tree, but the sky is different here... There was this private over there, young, right out of basic, tough guy, the neighborhood thug. We don't pull many like that any more. Well, this kid, this boy really, he couldn't have been more than eighteen, he's out there clowning around with his friends, having some beers. And he's got the tabs from the beer cans draped down his tee-shirt like a necklace. Just another bored-to-death boy, goofing his time away. So I took him downtown, but good. "That is your uniform, you lead head gyrene, whether you are on or off duty, and that is your motto on your stupid, ugly, mindless chest, Semper Fi. And you had better do some thinking with your little pea brain about what that means." And so on. You have to kick their ass sometimes. They expect it. It's what you do. That night we got hit. This boy was one of the wounded. He was still in his tee-shirt, covered with blood. I was kneeling over him. I don't know if he could see me, or if he even knew who I was, or if he was still in some dream in his sleep. He grabbed me tight, pulled me down. I could just barely hear him. "Semper Fi," he said, "Semper Fi." And I tried to talk to this boy. I said... I don't know what I said. He just kept repeating "Semper Fi. Semper Fi." And I wondered, what have I given this boy? And I held him. And he died. He deserved better. They all deserved better. *(Pause)*

ANNE: I'm sure it was a comfort to that boy that you held him. And I'm certain it was a comfort to those who loved him that he was not alone when he died. I'm going to go back in now. I'll see you in the morning. Goodnight, Owen.

OWEN: Goodnight, Anne. *(She exits.)* Dear God, Who gives order and purpose to this world, show me Your face, and show me the path through this darkness. Help me to know Your heart and Your will. And take me once again into Your love and Your peace. Let me know Your peace.

(The lights gradually fade. End of Act One.)

ACT TWO

Scene One

(On the large television monitor, a woman exercising. ANNE and AGNES are moving in time to insistent background music. Both are dressed in sweat pants and leotards. AGNES is in her mid-fifties, but appears younger, a woman who takes care of her body and her looks. She does the exercises with more ease than ANNE. It is early in the morning.)

EXERCISE WOMAN: ...right, right and more... and, yes, you can...

ANNE: ...and no, I can't...

EXERCISE WOMAN: ...eight and nine, come on!...

ANNE: ...go away! and eleven...

EXERCISE WOMAN: ...and twelve...

ANNE: ...and arghh!

EXERCISE WOMAN: Good! Good!

ANNE: That's it!

EXERCISE WOMAN: That's it!

ANNE: Isn't it funny, you can always tell what she's going to say next?

EXERCISE WOMAN: Now...

ANNE: I hate this part...

EXERCISE WOMAN: Hold it, and...

ANNE: Oh, God, no...

EXERCISE WOMAN: Go for the burn!

ANNE: ...oh please, not the burn.

EXERCISE WOMAN: You can!

ANNE: I can't! You want begging? I'll give you begging.

EXERCISE WOMAN: And hold it...

ANNE: ...That's easy for you to say...

EXERCISE WOMAN: And relax... *(The women stop the workout, AGNES quite gracefully, ANNE near collapse.)* And relax... and relax.

ANNE: Now, wasn't that good?

EXERCISE WOMAN: Now, wasn't that good? Move up to the sitting position. *(The women rise to a sitting posture.)* Come up slowly...

ANNE: *(Emitting enjoyable noises)* Ahhh, ohhh, hmmmm.

EXERCISE WOMAN: Breathe slowly, slowly, enjoy your breathing.

ANNE: Oh, Agnes, I'm having an out-of-body experience.

EXERCISE WOMAN: O.K., that's it. Breathe slow, sit for a bit. Remember...

ANNE and EXERCISE WOMAN: Do it good, and do it often.

ANNE: Pretty lewd advice, if you ask me.

EXERCISE WOMAN: And I'll see you tomorrow. Bye.

ANNE: Bye, y'all. *(The tape clicks off, the music slowly fades. ANNE moves the television out of view of the audience.)*

AGNES: You're getting better.

ANNE: Oh, stop.

AGNES: But you think too much. Just let it happen. But you're much better than when we started.

ACT TWO   37

ANNE: It's the company. Agnes, you're my living hope that we can retard the aging process.

(AGNES *crosses out to deck. She picks up a pair of binoculars which she uses to scan the horizon. She gathers a pail and some gardening tools from the kitchen.*)

ANNE: Any birds?

AGNES: Negative.

ANNE: How about men?

AGNES: *(Looking off)* I can see Arty. He's alone.

ANNE: *(Crossing to shrubs, preparing to weed and look for bugs.)* You think that's a good sign?

AGNES: *(Puts down binoculars.)* I don't know. So what do you think of himself?

ANNE: Hard to say. It's been all of one day, hasn't it?

AGNES: It took everything I had not to run over here last night. Just thinking about him gives me that tingle.

ANNE: That unmentionable tingle?

AGNES: Uh-huh.

ANNE: That's nice, Agnes.

AGNES: No, not nice. I'd say this tingle was damned inconvenient. Well, I'd better get cleaned up. I can't make the grand entrance looking like this. You didn't say anything about me and Phillip?

ANNE: Not a word. *(She exits.)*

AGNES: Good.

(ARTY *enters. He has been running full out. He stops, apart from the women, not noticing* AGNES. *He goes down to do push-ups, on his fingertips. After the first push-up he sees* AGNES. *Without a word he crosses to her, lifting her high in the air and twirling her around. She laughs, enjoying the attention.*)

AGNES: Well, look at you.

ARTY: Okay. You look fine, Mrs. C. You taking those pretty pills again?

AGNES: It's all natural. Arty you're a sight.

ARTY: How's the homecoming queen? Beverly High School, class of...

AGNES: Never mind what class. *(Sitting on the deck with him.)* You look good.

ARTY: I'm okay.

AGNES: We lost Timmy. I saw his name on the list. God, Arty, I'm so sorry.

ARTY: We had some times, didn't we?

AGNES: He was a good boy. Full of life and fun. A real good boy.

ARTY: He was the best... We had some times.

AGNES: I'm going to miss him. How is Owen taking it?

ARTY: I'm not sure.

AGNES: Is he pulling the old stone face on you?

ARTY: Yeah.

AGNES: The great Sphinx.

ARTY: He's keeping his own counsel.

AGNES: Oh, I know that one.

(BRIAN *enters, breathing heavily.*)

BRIAN: Mom. Mom! Mom? What are you doing here?

AGNES: *(Kissing him on the cheek.)* I'm doing my exercises and visiting with an old friend, that's what.

BRIAN: I thought you weren't going to show if Dad was here.

AGNES: Well, I changed my mind.

BRIAN: Mom, I'm not sure this is such a good idea.

AGNES: Don't get yourself all worked up, Brian.

ACT TWO

BRIAN: Dad's in a bad way, right now...

AGNES: And I've never seen him in a bad way? This is between your father and me, Brian.

BRIAN: Mom.

AGNES: Just stay out of the way.

BRIAN: Okay, okay. *(Stretching after his run)*

AGNES: *(Kissing* ARTY*)* I'm real glad you're back with us, Arty. Well, I've got to go make myself beautiful.

ARTY: Hey, don't do the job twice. (AGNES *exits.)*

BRIAN: *(Still stretching)* You're a runner.

ARTY: Nothing special.

BRIAN: No, it shows. You have form. I know. I have no form. You competed in college, right?

ARTY: No... Never went to college.

BRIAN: Oh.

ARTY: High school.

BRIAN: Track and field?

ARTY: And cross country. Now it's just part of the job.

BRIAN: *(Looking off)* He's pulled up.

ARTY: Hard to push yourself when you're being shoved.

BRIAN: You've been keeping an eye on him.

ARTY: Well, that's my job. And it's a two-way street. The colonel, he wants me to go permanent. He takes an interest, and I'm grateful. But then something happens, like this last time... I got my separation notice from Division. I've got to tell them if I'm going to keep wearing the uniform.

(ANNE *enters from the house.)*

ANNE: I just checked in with the station. Henry not only got us onto the base, but the network, God almighty, is going to take our feed live.

BRIAN: So you...?

ANNE: I do the coverage, nation-wide.

BRIAN: When does this happen?

ARTY: 1500 hours.

ANNE: Henry's calling to verify.

ARTY: Verify all you want. The bodies come in at 1500 hours. *(Pause)*

BRIAN: *(To* ARTY*)* Arty, I knew Tim and some of the others. I'd like to attend the ceremony, if it's open to the public.

ARTY: I'll get you clearance.

BRIAN: Thanks. *(He exits into the house.)*

ANNE: Look, Arty, I'm a news reporter. I look for stories. That's my job.

ARTY: Yeah, I noticed. Last I heard, the ceremony was closed door. No press.

ANNE: Well, I guess the powers that be want the official sanitized version to go out. Give America a good cry. Then let everybody forget.

ARTY: Yeah, that's usually how it works. *(Pause)*

ANNE: Just what was it you did over there, Arty? In the Root? Isn't that what the Marines call Beirut?

ARTY: Yeah, the Root.

ANNE: So?

ARTY: Colonel's ADC. Aide de camp.

ANNE: So you were the Colonel's right-hand man.

ARTY: Yeah.

ANNE: You could help him out. You must have been in on a lot of the planning. You knew the security arrangements, didn't you? *(Pause)* And I just stepped over the line, didn't I?

ACT TWO 41

ARTY: Yeah. Look, I would appreciate it if you would just back off. No questions about I what I did or what I knew, all right?

ANNE: Sorry. Arty, I'll be straight with you. If I could get an interview with someone who was over there, an eye-witness, that would be a big plus for me.

ARTY: Help you move right up the ladder.

ANNE: Yes it would. And the people over here, they have a right to know what's going on. So if you know someone...

ARTY: Someone?

ANNE: If you, or anyone you know, has something to say, just let me know, and I'll get the story out. And I protect my sources. *(Pause)*

ARTY: Well, I'll store that information.

ANNE: You're a careful man, Arthur, Arty Jenkins.

ARTY: Don't want to be quoted out of context.

(ARTY *exits. After a beat* ANNE *exits into the house. After a few seconds,* OWEN *enters walking. He positions himself to do a sit-up, thinks better of it, then changes to a push-up, on his finger tips. He holds the position for a moment, then relaxes into a sitting position.)*

OWEN: Do it. *(Gets into the push-up position.* BRIAN *re-enters, carrying a towel. He stops at the edge of the deck.)* Do it. A simple, mindless, exercise. Do it! (OWEN *does several push-ups, on his finger tips.)*

BRIAN: *(Crossing out to the deck)* Now that I can't do.

OWEN: Helps keep everything in neutral.

BRIAN: I'm impressed.

OWEN: Looks more impressive than it really is. Exercise without thought is posturing.

BRIAN: Oh yeah. *(Throws him the towel.)* Wipe it off.

OWEN: Conley's place looks the same. He still have those three pigs? What did he call them?

BRIAN: Breakfast, Lunch, and Dinner. Guess that helps him stay objective.

OWEN: You've done well out here, Brian.

BRIAN: I like what I do.

OWEN: Your Uncle Bewley says you saved a horse he would have destroyed.

BRIAN: Panache, yeah. Sometimes you get lucky.

OWEN: You fit in, like Bewley, and old man Conley with his farm. You've carved out a little slice of the world. You belong. That's the bottom line... When I called you, after the bombing, I forgot for a minute that your mother had left.

BRIAN: I figured.

OWEN: But I'm glad I reached you. We could always talk, you and I.

BRIAN: Yeah.

OWEN: Sukie's a girl. It's different. There's things you don't discuss with your daughter. Even when we talk Navy and Marines, there's things I can't say to her. And Bobby, well five minutes together in a room and well, I don't have to tell you.

BRIAN: You two will work it out, some day.

OWEN: He resents me. Always has. I think it all dates from those two years I was in Okinawa when he was a boy. He only got a piece of me, two little weeks in two long years. You were just a baby.

BRIAN: And always good tempered.

OWEN: Oh, I missed a lot of you, too. Your first steps, the first time you talked. Water under the family bridge, huh?

BRIAN: I've got no complaints. Then or any time since.

ACT TWO

OWEN: You were a quiet kid. You even cried quietly. For a while there your mother thought you were simple minded, or deaf or something.

BRIAN: What? I'm sorry, I couldn't quite hear...

OWEN: *(Throws the towel at* BRIAN.*)* When Bobby was born, I prayed to God, mister, make my son a Marine. And I hammered on that boy like I was God's anointed foreman. Kept at him till I drove him out of this house. That night when we got hit, pulling those poor boys out, prying them out, I realized that if God had heard my prayer, I might be digging my own son out of the rubble. So I believe that God does hear us. And He makes His adjustments... I've called your brother every day since I've been back. He doesn't answer his phone.

BRIAN: Yeah, he can be like that. Dad, Bobby's made it pretty clear to us. He doesn't want to see you again. I'm sorry. *(Pause)*

OWEN: I used to know where I stood, Brian. Then your mother left me, and all these insistent questions rolled in. I thought I wanted up and out, the pension and some pine trees. But the closer retirement got, the more nervous I got. The only thing I know is the Corps. The day-to-day civilian world is one big game show quiz to me. I just don't fit in. As a soldier I have a place, a position. And I like the life, the men. But if I can't do my job...

BRIAN: Who says you can't?

OWEN: I've been passed over for promotion once already. If my superiors wanted me to rise...

BRIAN: Then maybe your superiors don't know everything. You're talking politics.

OWEN: You may be right. Oh, Brian, I should have found a way, protected my men. I can't shake it.

BRIAN: You can't bring those men back to life, Dad. And there's nothing wrong with defending yourself. Dad, I called a lawyer for you, and I want you to talk to him.

OWEN: No, Brian. If it comes to that, Division will appoint counsel for me.

BRIAN: Well, he's available. Think about it. You know you've got a place here, whenever you want

OWEN: Thanks Brian, but I couldn't do that. This is your home now. Bewley's offered me the fishing lodge. You remember?

BRIAN: I know, by the lake. Look, Dad, I got some news. (AGNES *enters, no longer in sweat pants.*) That's the news. Hi, Mom. Well, I guess I'll just go and...yeah. *(He exits into the house.)*

AGNES: *(Embracing him)* I'm glad you're back.

OWEN: You look so fine, Aggs. So fine. *(Pause)*

AGNES: So?

OWEN: Had a talk with Brian. Been a while.

AGNES: You talked.

OWEN: We talked. He's doing fine. Well, you knew that. I like the girl.

AGNES: Lighten up, would you? This is me, Owen. I don't have horns and I didn't grow an extra eye. Don't go all strange on me.

OWEN: Now don't start that business again.

ANNE: The first two days after you come home you are the strangest man on the planet. You spend last night with the raccoons?

OWEN: It's different coming back, this time.

AGNES: I know. You had a real bad one over there.

OWEN: Not my fault.

ACT TWO 45

AGNES: Do you really think you have to tell me that?

OWEN: No. Sorry, Aggs. How's Phillip?

AGNES: Phil's all right. We get along. He's a phone call away and we don't ask too much of each other. You think about me?

OWEN: Every day. I was never straight with you, Aggs. I should have known I couldn't go civilian. I needed that full colonel before I dropped. I needed my wings. I don't blame you for taking the hike.

AGNES: I thought you'd hike right after me.

OWEN: Funny thing is, I could leave it now. *(Pause)* They've done well with the house. I almost didn't recognize the place at first, the new paint and everything.

AGNES: I couldn't stay here. Too many reminders. I've got a new place, pine trees in the back. The wind walks right through, every night.

OWEN: I'm glad you got your pine trees, Aggs.

AGNES: Owen, how are you taking all this other mess?

OWEN: I'm waiting for Division to call. And I'm trying not to end up on this year's political barbeque.

AGNES: Phil thinks you just might. And he's no dummy. The newspapers make it sound like you're at fault and no one in Washington is saying anything different.

OWEN: I know.

AGNES: That congressman owes you some favors.

OWEN: No, Aggs. You know I can't go over the head of my superiors.

AGNES: Even if they let you hang in the wind? They barbeque Boy Scouts too, you know. Stand up to them, Owen. You owe yourself that. And you owe it to Timmy and all the others.

OWEN: I've got to go through channels, Aggs. I don't know any other way. *(Pause)* Interest you in a little walk by the pond?

AGNES: No. Owen, I just wanted you to know that I'm glad you made it back... I've really got to go.

OWEN: Maybe we could give it another chance, Aggs. People do. And the Corps might be ready to dump me anyway.

AGNES: So you might as well have me?

OWEN: I didn't mean it like that.

AGNES: Sounds like that. Sounds like a second choice to me.

OWEN: Aggs, I haven't had a quiet day since you left me.

AGNES: I can't help that.

OWEN: And I've never stopped loving you. Not for one minute, one second. We should be like some old couple in the Bible, counting the nights, one by one. Maybe we could make a go of it.

AGNES: Not like this. Not with you waiting for the call, waiting to put on the harness. "Just this one time, Aggs, I swear. Then it's the promotion for sure. Then the pension, I promise. Just hang on."

OWEN: I did return, Aggs.

AGNES: Don't give me MacArthur, for God's sake.

OWEN: I think I could leave it now. Aggs, you've always been home for me.

AGNES: I can't Owen.

OWEN: Aggs...

AGNES: No. I promised myself I would never go down like one of those brittle and sad women who lose their husbands after the long haul, spending their lives building up a man to lose him to fatigue or to some piece of fluff...

OWEN: Never, Aggs, never.

ACT TWO   47

AGNES: No, I know that...But we had a bargain, Owen. All those years, waiting for the phone to ring, or Vietnam, praying it wouldn't, with you in all those places with names I couldn't even say straight. You've done every duty in the book. You've been their mule, always ready to pull the load without complaining. You've covered for the Corps and now they are letting you go hang...

OWEN: I don't know that for a fact.

AGNES: Letting you hang in the wind. Will you finally open your eyes, Owen. You had to have the promotion, the hazardous duty to have the promotion. Well, it cost you Bobby, and it cost us our marriage. And they are going to chuck you away. *(Pause)* I'm sorry, Owen. I didn't come here to open old wounds. I'm glad you didn't get hurt. I've got my pine trees. Goodbye, Owen.

OWEN: I love you, Aggs, always will.

(BRIAN *enters, in the house, looking out to the deck.*)

AGNES: If only you had loved me more than that damn promotion.

OWEN: I need you, Aggs. I need you.

AGNES: Oh God, no!

(*She exits, running past the shrubs.* BRIAN *crosses to the deck.*)

BRIAN: Dad?

OWEN: Your mother is a good woman, Brian. The best there is. The salt of the earth. I've lost her. Lost Bobby. Lost everything, everyone.

BRIAN: You haven't lost me.

OWEN: What in hell did I ever give you? A couple of weeks a year? A man should give more to his son.

BRIAN: It doesn't matter. That's over. Past history.

OWEN: Your mother told me to fight them. Isn't that amazing? Telling me to fight?

BRIAN: Then that's what we're going to do. Dad, talk to the lawyer.

OWEN: I don't have any fight left in me, son.

BRIAN: No way. You're Owen Corbett. You're the CO, the man in charge. You're my father. Don't let them do this to you, Dad. Dad?

OWEN: Got to take a little walk. Got to clear my head.

(OWEN *exits past the hedge.* BRIAN *remains on stage, crossing into the house as the lights shift.)*

Scene Two

(Evening. The stage is empty. The sound of a drum roll is heard from the television, which is turned away from the audience. ANNE *enters and sits with* BRIAN. ARTY *enters and crosses to the deck. He is in military dress: shoes, pants and sweater. From the television we hear* ANNE's *voice.)*

ANNE: *(V.O. television)* And now the last of the coffins. Accompanied by the same measured careful step. The same precise honor guard.

(BRIAN *and* OWEN *enter,* OWEN *in military dress. The drumming ends. A trumpet sounds taps, the final note lingering.)*

ANNE: *(V.O. television)* This concludes our coverage of the Marine... *(She points a remote control at the television, cutting off the program.)*

BRIAN: That was good work.

ANNE: Sometimes all you have to do is point the camera. I'm still surprised the network let me cover.

BRIAN: You're a rising star.

ANNE: Yeah. *(Crossing to trolley bar, pouring herself a drink)* I didn't realize there would be so many bodies. I thought they'd just keep bringing them in. That it would never end. Body after body. *(Crossing to* ARTY *on the deck)* Arty, I didn't know.

ARTY: Now you do. I should have been in that building. That was my station. But we had visiting dignitaries. If I had been sleeping like the others...

BRIAN: *(Offers* ARTY *a glass.)* How about a drink, Arty?

ARTY: Thanks.

ARTY: They never knew what hit them. Some people think that's the way to go. I think it's the worst. To go to sleep and never wake up. God damn. I knew them. I dug them out. I put them in their body bags. Then you're supposed to stand there and take it, at attention, like some statue. Like it's just rolling off you. God damn. God damn. God damn.

(OWEN *enters from the house.*)

OWEN: *(To* ANNE*)* Your people did a fine job, Anne.

ANNE: Thank you, Owen. I'd like to tell the crew you said that, down at the station.

OWEN: You tell them it was appreciated. Well, I guess I know where I stand with Division.

(The telephone rings, a modern, chirping sound. BRIAN *crosses to the study.)*

OWEN: Not one damned word. No one even had the kindness to call me a son of a bitch.

BRIAN: *(Re-entering, to* OWEN*)* It's for you. A Mr. Harper from Washington.

(OWEN *crosses into the study; a long pause.)*

OWEN: *(Returning to the deck)* Mr. Harper would like to talk to me tomorrow morning. Mr. Harper scurries between the departments of State and Defense, handling delicate foreign issues. Which I guess is what I am. He wouldn't say more. Mr. Harper is a civilian... Well? Arty, the uniform is off.

ARTY: They're setting you up, Sir.

ANNE: Absolutely.

BRIAN: It looks that way, Dad.

ARTY: Damn, it would serve this civilian, all these civilians, right if they got a real ugly, dirty war dropped right in their lap, right here. Show them the real price of their carelessness. Their damned carelessness.

ACT TWO

ANNE: Owen, I can have major media here in four hours. Guaranteed.

OWEN: Go public?

ANNE: I can arrange an anonymous leak, with your story, your words.

ARTY: That might be the way, Sir.

OWEN: I'd have to resign my commission.

ANNE: If you resign the world reads that as guilt.

ARTY: I agree, Sir.

BRIAN: Dad, before you do anything, please, please talk to this lawyer.

ANNE: Owen, don't let them get away with this.

BRIAN: Dad, the lawyer...

OWEN: Enough. Enough... Those men were my responsibility in the eyes of God. I will find my way through this. *(He moves toward the house;* ARTY *stands and starts to follow.)*

ARTY: Sir, I'd like to ...

OWEN: No, Arty. This one I do alone. *(He exits.)*

ARTY: You know what the Marines say?

BRIAN: What's that, Arty?

ARTY: We return for our dead. That's who we are. Well, we brought them back. Now, won't someone tell me, what exactly did they die for?

*(*ARTY *exits. The lights shift around* BRIAN *and* ANNE, *who remain on stage. Lights down.)*

Scene Three

(The following morning. HARPER *and* GENERAL DAVIS *enter.* OWEN *enters into the study. He is in full dress blues. After a beat,* ANNE *exits.)*

BRIAN: I'll tell my father you're here. *(He crosses in to* OWEN.*)* They're all yours. *(He exits into the house.* OWEN *crosses to the deck.)*

OWEN: General Davis.

DAVIS: Owen.

OWEN: Mr. Harper.

HARPER: Good morning, Colonel. Nice place you have here.

*(*ARTY *enters, in full dress uniform. He salutes* GENERAL DAVIS.*)*

DAVIS: As you were, Lieutenant.

OWEN: Lieutenant Jenkins, I'd like you to witness this conversation.

ARTY: Yes, Sir.

HARPER: This conversation is closed and classified, Colonel.

OWEN: The Lieutenant handles my private and professional correspondence. He has the highest security clearance.

HARPER: Well, if you are willing to vouch for the Lieutenant.

OWEN: I just did, didn't I?

HARPER: Well, Colonel, as I told you on the phone, we've just come from a policy review at State.

OWEN: The State Department.

ACT TWO   53

HARPER: There's also Defense, your people, our allies. It gets complicated.

OWEN: Why don't you stop crapping around and say what you came to say. Because if you came here for my resignation, you don't have it. And if this goes to a court martial, I will defend myself and the integrity of my command, fully and completely.

HARPER: Wait, wait a minute. That's not what this is about.

OWEN: Then what the hell is this about?

HARPER: This is about, Colonel, your position as commander of our forces...

OWEN: Which is something you know nothing about, nothing at all, Mr. Harper. *(To* DAVIS*)* What is he talking about?

DAVIS: Mr. Harper and I are both here for the same reason, Owen.

HARPER: You might try listening to me, Colonel. You know, the book on you says straight arrow all the way, a Company man. I'm not surprised, considering that evaluation comes from military intelligence.

DAVIS: You had better stop right there, Mister, while you still have a mouth in working order.

HARPER: Let's just back this up. I haven't had a whole lot of sleep in the last few days. *(To* OWEN*)* If it takes the General here playing Dirty Harry with my face, okay. New security measures are in place. Colonel, we just want you back in command.

OWEN: In command?

HARPER: There is an ongoing re-examination of the rules of engagement.

OWEN: *(To* DAVIS*)* This isn't a hatchet job?

DAVIS: Re-instatement of command, effective immediately.

OWEN: *(To* DAVIS*)* Why doesn't Division just order me back?

DAVIS: Division isn't running the show any more.

HARPER: You were pulled out by the military command, Colonel. A number of decisions by that command are under review. Meanwhile we need someone over there who has the confidence of the troops. The book says that's you. How about it?

OWEN: *(Laughing)* Re-instatement of command? Now that is not what I expected, no. No, I've been sitting here, just waiting for you and General Davis to hand me my head.

HARPER: Colonel, we're not ...

OWEN: You see, Mr. Harper, after thirty years I have a wife who can't live with me, one son I barely know, and another who treats me like an infectious disease. And a daughter, yes, who is willing to risk being blown out of the water to make sure I pay some attention to her. Now that is one hell of a life summary, don't you think?

HARPER: Colonel, we are on a very tight schedule.

OWEN: To hell with your schedule! You take some of your precious time and learn something here. Something you can take back to your damn committee.

HARPER: Colonel, my report will indicate that you requested changes in your level of security, and changes in the rules of engagement. You're clean, Colonel.

OWEN: I don't feel clean! *(To* DAVIS*)* Is that it, Sam? Oil the machine, jump back on the bus? Is that the message from Washington?

DAVIS: With your name cleared. What more do you want?

OWEN: I want some satisfaction. I want some explanation.

DAVIS: No. You just want your pound of flesh.

OWEN: Maybe I do. You should have backed me, Sam.

ACT TWO

DAVIS: And what good would that have done? This was a diplomatic dog and pony show.

OWEN: You could have changed those damn orders of engagement.

DAVIS: That was a political decision.

OWEN: And you have the political connections.

DAVIS: God almighty, man, we are not in some puking banana republic where the government is our personal property. The civilians decide the policy, and we do the work. Tinker with that and it's chaos, Owen. Now you can resign, my friend, have your moment in front of the cameras, and be old news in three days. Or you can help us pick up the pieces... For once will you read between the lines? Someone else is going to hang. Right, Mr. Harper?

HARPER: The committee has not yet reached a finding.

DAVIS: But I appear to be the people's choice. Or should I say, your choice?

HARPER: Any conclusions at this point are preliminary.

DAVIS: Preliminary, my ass, Mister. I am not going to take the fall for this. You had better understand that. And you had damn well understand who you are dealing with.

HARPER: I understand who I'm dealing with. And why I'm here. Not to listen to you, General. I've already heard what you've had to say. I'm here, we're both here, to retrieve Colonel Corbett. *(Pause)*

DAVIS: How about it, Owen? We have a mother of a morale problem over there. Come back on board. Resume command.

OWEN: I can't do it, Sam. I can't face the men.

DAVIS: Funny thing about that. The word over there is that you went up against the brass to change the rules of engagement. *(To* ARTY*)* Any idea, Lieutenant, how a story like that could get around?

ARTY: Difficult to say, Sir.

DAVIS: I bet it is, Lieutenant.

HARPER: Colonel, the committee is aware that you will be returning under less than optimal conditions. We can justify a bump up in rank.

OWEN: What?

HARPER: A promotion, Colonel. I don't want there to be any misunderstanding because you and I didn't hit it off.

OWEN: Is that what the book says on me? Dangle the promotion and I jump through the hoop?

HARPER: I'm not going by the book, Colonel. Let's just call this an adjustment in rank.

OWEN: Screw you. Who the hell do you think you are? I should smash your damn face in.

HARPER: Colonel, I just thought...

OWEN: Screw your promotion. Screw it! Screw it! You hear me?

DAVIS: Owen...

OWEN: And screw you too, Sam. This isn't about a promotion. What about my command? I must be able to protect my men.

DAVIS: Owen, your entire unit is going to be re-deployed.

OWEN: Re-deployed?

HARPER: To naval vessels off the coast.

(ANNE *enters from the house, crossing to* BRIAN *in the study.*)

OWEN: And would you tell me, Mr. Harper, just how that will improve our presence among the local population?

HARPER: The policy is evolving, Colonel.

OWEN: You don't have a policy. Our government doesn't have a policy. And my men died because you make it up as

ACT TWO 57

you go along. You just remember that, Mr. Harper, the next time your damn committee determines policy. *(Pause)*

HARPER: Colonel, the offer of a promotion was clearly a mistake, and that offer is withdrawn. But we do need to know, will you resume command?

OWEN: I have to think.

DAVIS: Owen...

OWEN: I need a minute. You can give me a damn minute.

DAVIS: Mr. Harper, I am going to go through that gate and walk north. I suggest that you walk south. And I will meet you at the car in five minutes.

(HARPER *exits.*)

OWEN: That son of a bitch destroyed my command. And you didn't do a damned thing to prevent it. You just played their game of images and impressions. And you made me play the game. I was your boy, wasn't I, Sam?

DAVIS: How many times do I have to say this? The government wanted a dog and pony show, pure and simple.

OWEN: Well, they got that. You were their dog, and I was your pony.

DAVIS: You are way out of line, Colonel.

OWEN: You just let it happen. And so did I.

DAVIS: You have five minutes. *(He exits.* ARTY *salutes.)*

OWEN: Arty?

ARTY: Sir?

OWEN: Sound the all clear.

(ARTY *crosses into the house; after a beat,* ANNE *and* BRIAN *enter.)*

OWEN: They want me to go back. They want me to resume command.

BRIAN: That's great, Dad.

ANNE: Don't do it, Owen. They'll run you up the flagpole and sweep the blood under the carpet. Just business as usual. Like it never happened.

BRIAN: Annie, Annie...

OWEN: We're family, Brian. Let Annie have her say.

ANNE: They're using you. They are using you and Arty like pieces in some gray game. You're not on the beach at Normandy, Owen. Can't you see it? You're their cover. The gentleman soldier who played by the rules. Don't go back there. You don't belong.

OWEN: And just where do I belong? Where on God's earth do I belong? Would you tell me that? Not back on the base. Not here. And not with Agnes... I brought those men in. I just wanted to get them home in one piece. That's where I belong.

ANNE: Go public, Owen. Stand in front of the cameras. Tell your story. Tell the story of those men. Make someone be responsible. *(Pause)*

OWEN: I can't go that route, Anne.

ANNE: No, I guess you can't. What would Agnes say to you, if she were here?

BRIAN: Keep your head down, and don't be a hero.

OWEN: Right. Anne, would you do me a favor?

ANNE: If I can.

OWEN: When you see Agnes, would you tell her the mule has one last load to pull?

ANNE: That's all?

OWEN: She knows the rest.

(ARTY *enters, carrying duffel bags.*)

ANNE: Arty, Arthur Jenkins, be careful.

ARTY: I'll do my best. You say goodbye to Mrs. C. for me.

ACT TWO

ANNE: I certainly will.

OWEN: *(To* BRIAN*)* Not much of a visit.

BRIAN: Just like old times. No, better than old times.

OWEN: When I get back Brian, I want to see your brother. I want you and I to go out there.

BRIAN: I don't think Bobby will talk to you, Dad.

OWEN: I have to reconcile with the boy. Will you come with me, knock on his door?

BRIAN: If I do that, Bobby might never talk to me again.

OWEN: I know what I'm asking of you, Son. *(Pause)*

BRIAN: All right, Dad. I'll go with you.

OWEN: And then I want us to fix up the fishing lodge. I want to plant pine trees, you and me. And I want you to build me a deck, just like this one. I...goodbye, Son.

BRIAN: Goodbye, Dad. *(They embrace.)* Arty?

ARTY: *(Shaking hands)* Thanks again

OWEN: *(To* ANNE*)* Annie, thanks for putting up with us.

ANNE: *(Embracing him)* Keep your head down, and don't be a hero.

(ANNE *and* BRIAN *cross into the house, remaining visible.)*

ARTY: *(Putting down duffel bags)* Sir? Colonel?

OWEN: What's on your mind, Lieutenant?

ARTY: Well, Sir, when we get back to the base...

OWEN: What do you want to say, Arty?

ARTY: Sir, I'm not going to re-enlist. I won't be going back with you over there.

OWEN: You're sure on this, Son?

ARTY: I am.

OWEN: Well, Arty, I wish you the best of everything. If there's anything I can do, don't hesitate.

ARTY: Thank you, Sir. Semper Fi, Colonel.

OWEN: Semper Fi, Lieutenant.

(ARTY *exits.*)

OWEN: Semper Fi.

(OWEN *remains on stage. The lights gradually fade.*)

CURTAIN

www.ingramcontent.com/pod-product-compliance
Lightning Source LLC
Chambersburg PA
CBHW072015060426
42446CB00043B/2553